ELC

THE USBORNE BOOK OF
ORIGAMI

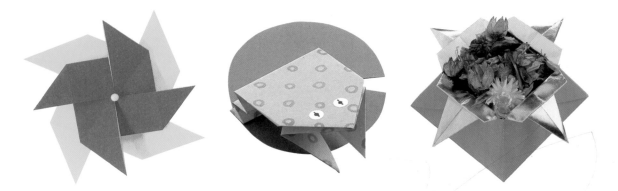

Eileen O'Brien and Kate Needham

Edited by Fiona Watt
Designed by Rachel Wells
Illustrated by John Woodcock
Photographs by Howard Allman and Ray Moller

Contents

Getting started	2	Beads	18
Hats	4	Star box	20
Glider	6	Bombs away	22
Fox family	8	Lily	24
Snapping mouths	10	Flapping bird	26
Snake fangs	12	Christmas tree	28
Big bang	13	Star	30
Jumping frogs	14	Other ideas	31
Windmills	16	Preliminary base	32

Series editor: Cheryl Evans • Managing designer: Mary Cartwright
Origami consultant: Sarah Goodall • Additional ideas: Ray Gibson

Getting started

Origami is a Japanese word which means 'paper folding'. Traditional origami models are not decorated in any way. The whole model is made by folding paper only.

In this book however, you will find ideas for decorating the folded paper by cutting, gluing or drawing things on the model.

Use newspaper, or pages from old magazines or comics.

You could decorate paper with felt-tip pens.

This origami lily is a traditional model, but it has a straw for a stem.

What kind of paper?

You can buy special paper for origami from art and craft stores, and Japanese stores. It is thin and easy to fold. You can also use the different types of paper shown here. For most projects, you will need scissors and a ruler.

Gift wrap works for most models.

This lily has been decorated with spots.

You can see how to make these lilies on pages 24-25.

Folding tips

Here are some basic tips to remember when folding paper:

1. Always work on a hard, flat surface.

2. Make sure that the corners and edges of the paper meet before you press the fold flat.

3. Press down on the middle of the fold first, and then smooth firmly out to the sides.

Hold the edges together firmly.

Symbols used in this book

Symbols are used in most of the projects to help you follow each step.

You can see the main ones used throughout the book below:

 This curly arrow means turn the paper over.

 This symbol means turn the paper upside down.

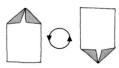

– – – This shows you where to make a fold, or where the paper has already been folded.

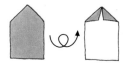

 Fold the paper in the direction shown by the arrow.

 Fold and then unfold the paper to make a crease.

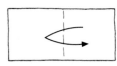

If you haven't tried origami before, start with the projects at the beginning of this book, as they get more difficult as the book goes on.

3

Hats

These bright hats are great for parties or for dressing up. You could decorate them like the ones shown in the pictures below.

You will need for the crown: four squares of paper 20 x 20cm (8 x 8in). Gift wrap is good. **For the party hat**: a 48 x 48cm (19 x 19in) square piece of paper.

Crown

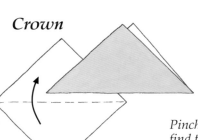

1. Place the paper on a table wrong side up, with one corner facing you. Fold the top and bottom corners together. Crease the middle.

Glue on sequins and paper diamond shapes.

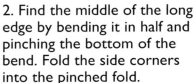

Pinch here to find the middle.

Pinched fold

2. Find the middle of the long edge by bending it in half and pinching the bottom of the bend. Fold the side corners into the pinched fold.

3. Fold all the other squares in the same way. Then stand them in a square with the corners pointing in, ready to join them together.

The folds meet here.

When you have completed your crown, add some tape on the inside.

4. Make the crown by slotting each corner inside the next one, making sure that the folds meet. The last corner slots into the first one.

Party hat

1. Lay the paper on a flat surface, with its wrong side facing up, and with one corner pointing at you.

2. Bring the top corner down to meet the bottom corner and crease the middle fold very neatly.

3. Fold the top right corner across to the left side of the paper so that the edges shown above are parallel.

These edges must be parallel, which means at the same angle.

The edges meet here.

4. Now fold the top left corner across to the opposite side in the same way. Check that the bottom edges meet.

For a bird's beak, in step 5, don't fold up the second triangle.

Glue on a skull and crossbones.

Glue some crepe paper strips for hair to the inside of a clown hat.

Bottom triangle

5. Fold the top layer only of the bottom triangle up over the edges. Turn the paper over and repeat.

Glider

This glider flies through the air when you throw it in a straight line, and dives down dramatically when you throw it up in the air.
You will need: a rectangle of paper 30 x 21cm (11 x 8in). Writing paper, gift wrap, an old magazine or newspaper, works for this origami model.

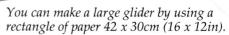

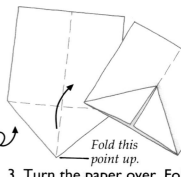

You can make a large glider by using a rectangle of paper 42 x 30cm (16 x 12in).

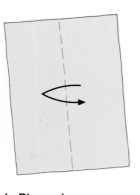

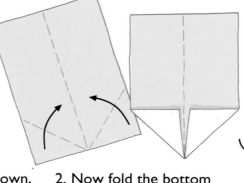

Fold this point up.

1. Place the paper as shown, with the right side up. Fold the long edges together and unfold them again.

2. Now fold the bottom corners in to make triangles so that the bottom edges meet the middle crease.

3. Turn the paper over. Fold up the bottom point as shown above, and crease the fold well.

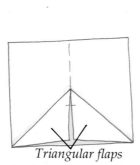

Triangular flaps

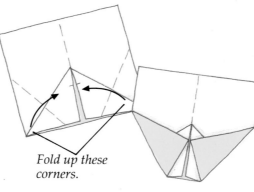

Fold up these corners.

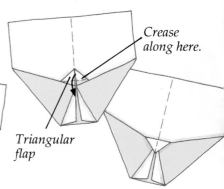

Crease along here.

Triangular flap

4. Mark a point about a third of the way down the triangular flaps, as shown in the picture above.

5. Fold in the bottom corners of the paper so that they meet at this point. Crease the folds well.

6. Fold the top point of the triangular flap down as far as it will go, over the triangles made in step 5.

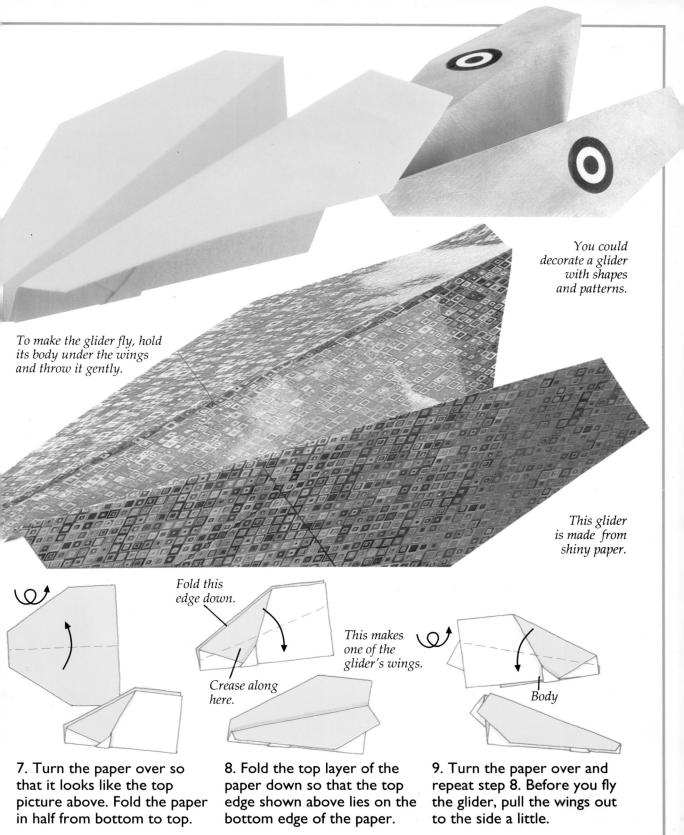

You could decorate a glider with shapes and patterns.

To make the glider fly, hold its body under the wings and throw it gently.

This glider is made from shiny paper.

Fold this edge down.

Crease along here.

This makes one of the glider's wings.

Body

7. Turn the paper over so that it looks like the top picture above. Fold the paper in half from bottom to top.

8. Fold the top layer of the paper down so that the top edge shown above lies on the bottom edge of the paper.

9. Turn the paper over and repeat step 8. Before you fly the glider, pull the wings out to the side a little.

7

Fox family

These foxes are easy to fold. You can make a whole family of foxes by using the paper sizes given on the opposite page. You could use gift wrap or decorate your own paper before you fold it.

You will need: a square piece of paper, 15 x 15cm (6 x 6in) is a good size to start with.

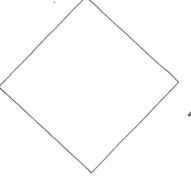

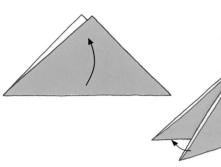

1. Place the paper on a flat surface with its wrong side facing up. Turn it so that one corner is pointing down.

2. Fold the bottom corner to the top and crease along the middle. Now fold it in half from right to left.

Fold up one layer only.

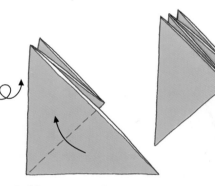

3. Bring the top layer of the bottom left corner up to meet the top point. Make sure all the edges meet.

4. Now turn the paper over and repeat step 3 very neatly on the other side, as shown in the picture above.

You could use spotted or striped paper.

Use a thick felt-tip pen to draw stripes.

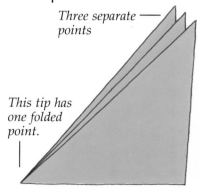

Three separate points

This tip has one folded point.

5. Place the triangle as shown above, with the longest edge on the left and the tip with three points, at the top.

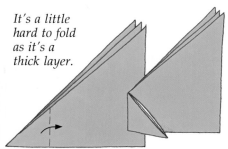

*It's a little
hard to fold
as it's a
thick layer.*

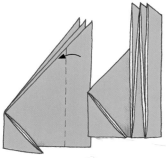

6. To make the tail, fold the bottom left corner as shown by the dotted line and arrow in the picture above.

7. Continue by folding all the layers of the right side over to the left so that they meet the tip of the tail.

To make a family

Use different sizes of paper for various members of the family. Try the sizes given below.
Large fox: 15 x 15cm (6 x 6in).
Medium fox: 12 x 12cm (5 x 5in).
Fox cub: 7.5 x 7.5cm (3 x 3in).

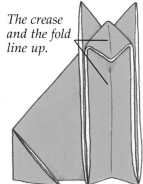

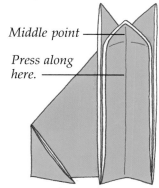

Middle point

Press along here.

8. Now separate the layers of paper in the flap you folded in the last step so that there are four layers on each side.

9. Press along the middle fold with your finger so that both of the flaps lie flat. The middle point will not lie flat.

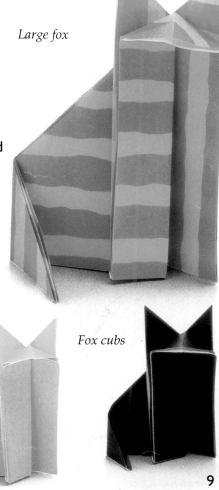

Large fox

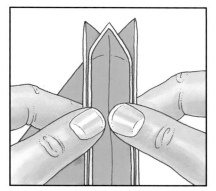

*The crease
and the fold
line up.*

*Medium
fox*

Fox cubs

10. To make the fox's head, squash the middle point flat. The crease in the head lines up with the middle fold.

9

Snapping mouths

You can decorate these snapping mouths, by using the ideas below, to make lots of different types of birds and animals. **You will need**: a square piece of paper 20 x 20cm (8 x 8in). Strong paper such as thick writing paper works best.

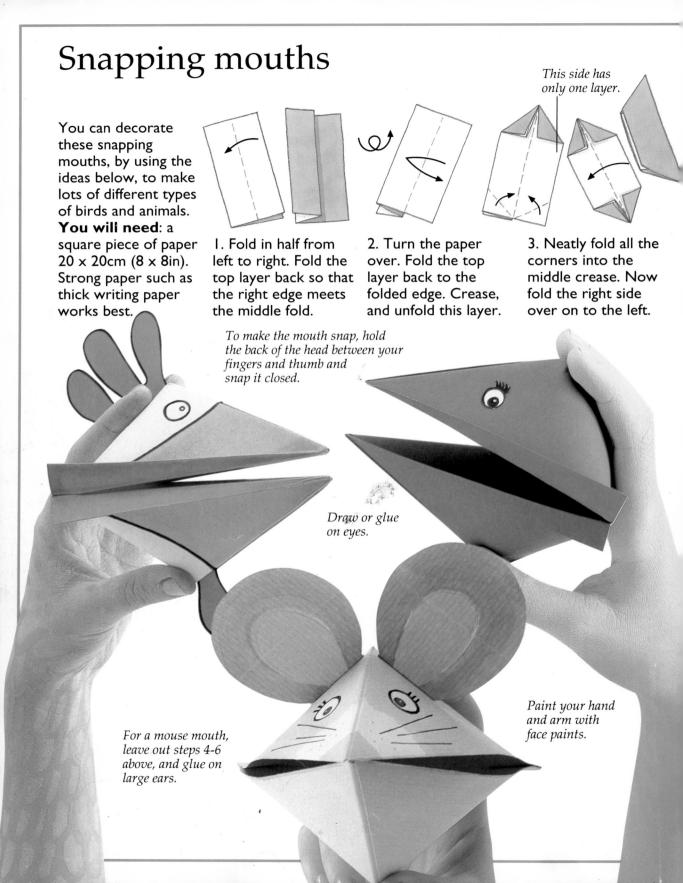

This side has only one layer.

1. Fold in half from left to right. Fold the top layer back so that the right edge meets the middle fold.

2. Turn the paper over. Fold the top layer back to the folded edge. Crease, and unfold this layer.

3. Neatly fold all the corners into the middle crease. Now fold the right side over on to the left.

To make the mouth snap, hold the back of the head between your fingers and thumb and snap it closed.

Draw or glue on eyes.

For a mouse mouth, leave out steps 4-6 above, and glue on large ears.

Paint your hand and arm with face paints.

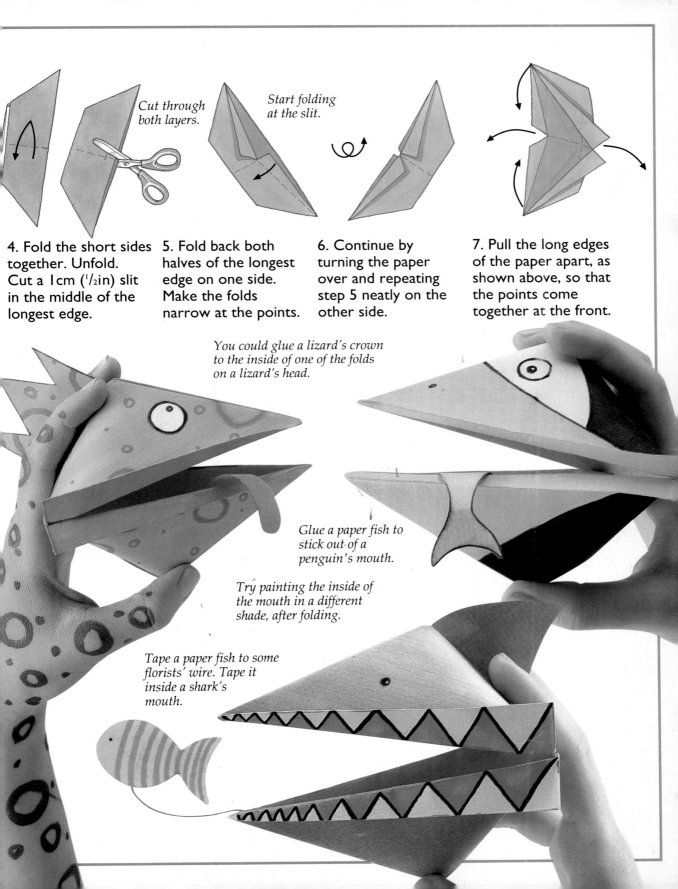

4. Fold the short sides together. Unfold. Cut a 1cm (½in) slit in the middle of the longest edge.

Cut through both layers.

Start folding at the slit.

5. Fold back both halves of the longest edge on one side. Make the folds narrow at the points.

6. Continue by turning the paper over and repeating step 5 neatly on the other side.

7. Pull the long edges of the paper apart, as shown above, so that the points come together at the front.

You could glue a lizard's crown to the inside of one of the folds on a lizard's head.

Glue a paper fish to stick out of a penguin's mouth.

Try painting the inside of the mouth in a different shade, after folding.

Tape a paper fish to some florists' wire. Tape it inside a shark's mouth.

Snake fangs

You will need: a rectangle of paper twice as long as it is wide, for example, 6 x 12cm (2½x 5in). Use paper that is white on one side.

Wear a sock on your hand for a snake's body.

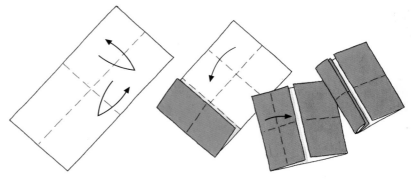

1. With the white side up, fold the long edges together and crease. Unfold. Fold the short edges together in the same way. Then unfold them.

2. Fold both of the short edges into the middle crease. Now fold the left edge only into the middle again and crease the fold.

Fold this corner.

This edge lies along the crease made in step 3.

These are the fangs.

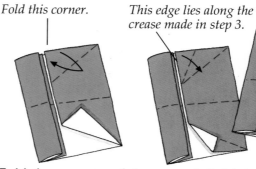

3. Fold the corners of the right side toward the middle. Try to fold more or less as shown in the picture above. Unfold them again.

4. Fold the same corners over to meet the creases made in step 3. Then fold the triangles over, along the creases made in step 3.

Glue or sew on eyes.

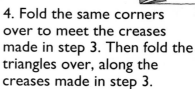

Fold this edge down.

To open and close the fangs, hold them at the corners and squeeze gently.

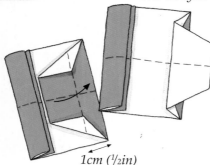

1cm (½in)

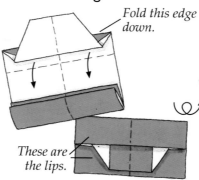

These are the lips.

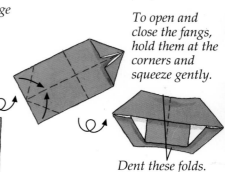

Dent these folds.

5. Now bend the top flap over the right edge, making a crease around 1cm (½in) from the edge, as shown in the picture above.

6. Place the paper as shown. Fold the top of the paper down to the middle so that the lips meet and the white fangs stick out.

7. Turn the paper over and fold all the corners into the middle crease. Shape the lips by denting the top and bottom folds.

Big bang

When you hold this banger at one corner and snap it down quickly, it makes a very loud noise. Thin gift wrap or a sheet of newspaper makes a really loud bang.

You will need: a large rectangle of thin paper, for example, a piece 37 x 50cm (15 x 20in).

Glue on lightning flashes and stars.

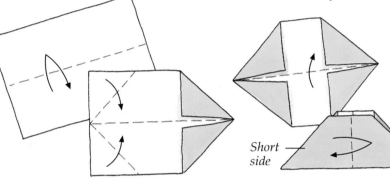

Short side

1. With the wrong side up, fold the longest sides of the paper together and crease. Unfold. Fold all the corners into the middle crease.

2. Fold the paper in half along the middle crease. With the long side at the bottom, fold the short sides together and unfold them again.

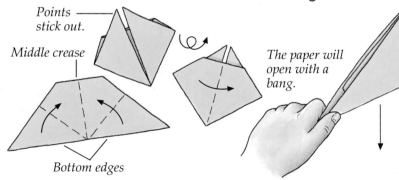

Points stick out.

Middle crease

The paper will open with a bang.

Bottom edges

3. Fold up both bottom corners so that the bottom edges meet the middle crease. Turn the paper over. Fold in half from side to side.

4. With the long edge facing you, hold the banger at the open end. Then put your hand in the air and bring it down sharply.

You could use striped paper.

13

Jumping frogs

These leaping frogs can jump high into the air. You could cut out a large circle for a pond, and smaller circles for lily pads. Try jumping your frogs onto the lily pads.
You will need: a rectangle of paper 8 x 13cm (3 x 5in); red, blue and yellow felt-tip pens. Thick writing paper or an old birthday card is ideal to use, as it's quite springy.

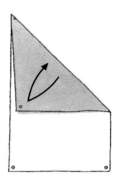

1. Mark the corners of the paper on both sides in red and blue as shown in the picture above.

2. With the wrong side up, fold one blue corner across to the opposite edge. Unfold it again.

Lay the paper flat when you have unfolded it.

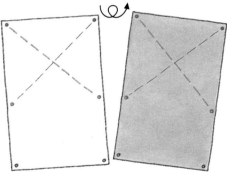

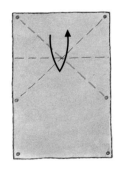

3. Now fold the other blue corner across to the opposite side in the same way and unfold it.

4. Mark the ends of the new creases (made in steps 2 and 3) yellow on both sides of the paper as shown above.

5. With the right side up, fold the edge with the blue corners down to the yellow marks. Now unfold it.

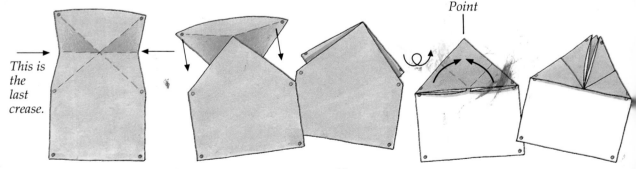

This is the last crease.

Point

6. Put a finger at each end of the last crease and push gently inward. The middle should pop up.

7. Flatten the blue corners down behind so that they touch the yellow marks. Press this flap flat underneath.

8. Turn the paper over and fold the blue corners up to the point. This makes the front feet.

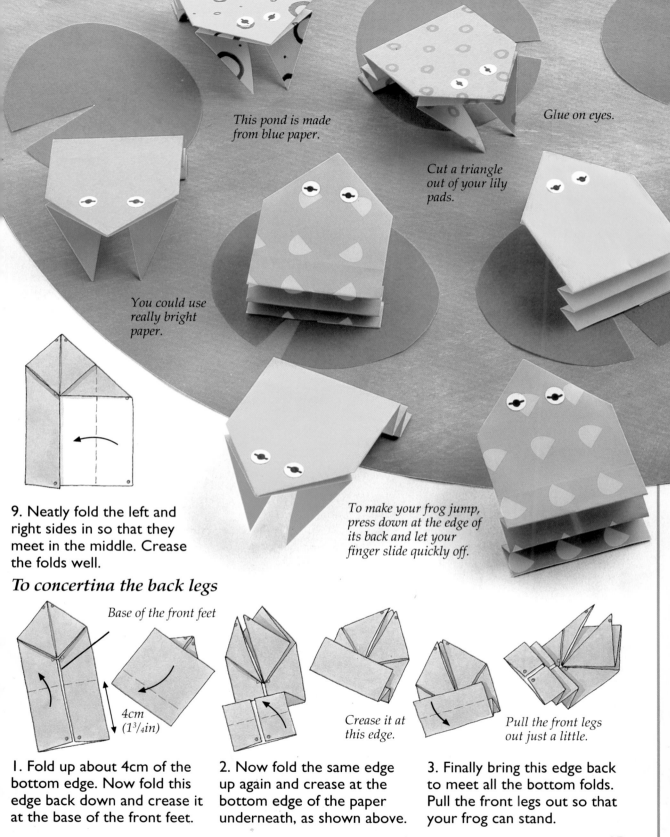

This pond is made
from blue paper.

Glue on eyes.

Cut a triangle
out of your lily
pads.

You could use
really bright
paper.

9. Neatly fold the left and
right sides in so that they
meet in the middle. Crease
the folds well.

To make your frog jump,
press down at the edge of
its back and let your
finger slide quickly off.

To concertina the back legs

Base of the front feet

4cm
(1³/₄in)

Crease it at
this edge.

Pull the front legs
out just a little.

1. Fold up about 4cm of the
bottom edge. Now fold this
edge back down and crease it
at the base of the front feet.

2. Now fold the same edge
up again and crease at the
bottom edge of the paper
underneath, as shown above.

3. Finally bring this edge back
to meet all the bottom folds.
Pull the front legs out so that
your frog can stand.

15

Windmills

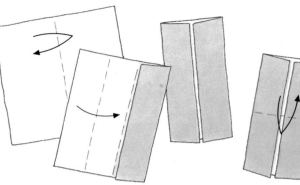

These windmills spin when you blow them or walk with them in a breeze. You could decorate your windmill using the ideas below.

You will need: a square piece of paper 15 x 15cm (6 x 6in); a thin green garden stick, or a kebab stick; a thumbtack or pinboard pin. Light paper, such as thin gift wrap, spins very well.

1. With the wrong side of the paper facing you, fold two edges together and unfold. Now fold these edges into the middle crease.

2. Fold the short edges together and unfold them. Now fold the short edges into the middle crease. This makes two flaps.

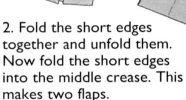

Top flap

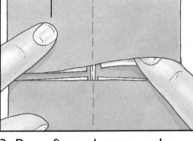

Placing your fingers on this side keeps the paper in place.

3. Put a finger between the two layers of the right side of the top flap. Hold the left side of the flap to keep the paper in place.

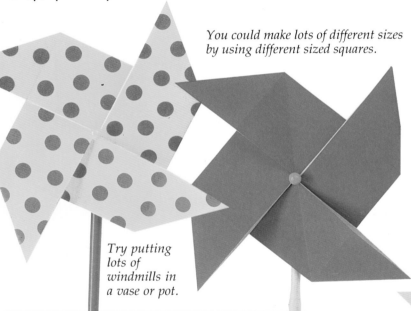

You could make lots of different sizes by using different sized squares.

Try putting lots of windmills in a vase or pot.

To attach a windmill to a stick

Push a thumbtack or pinboard pin through the middle of a windmill. Push the pin through your stick, close to the top. Leave enough room for the windmill to spin around the pin.

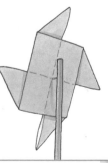

Make a double windmill by putting a smaller windmill in front. Use a square of paper 2.5cm (1in) smaller than the first square.

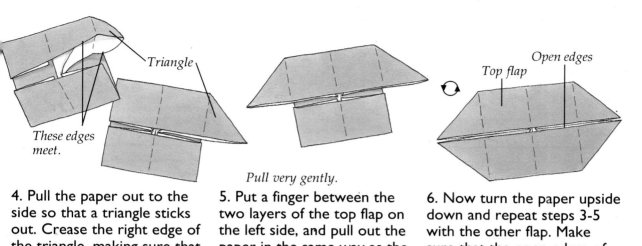

Triangle

Top flap *Open edges*

These edges meet.

Pull very gently.

4. Pull the paper out to the side so that a triangle sticks out. Crease the right edge of the triangle, making sure that the bottom edges meet.

5. Put a finger between the two layers of the top flap on the left side, and pull out the paper in the same way as the right flap in step 4.

6. Now turn the paper upside down and repeat steps 3-5 with the other flap. Make sure that the open edges of both flaps meet in the middle.

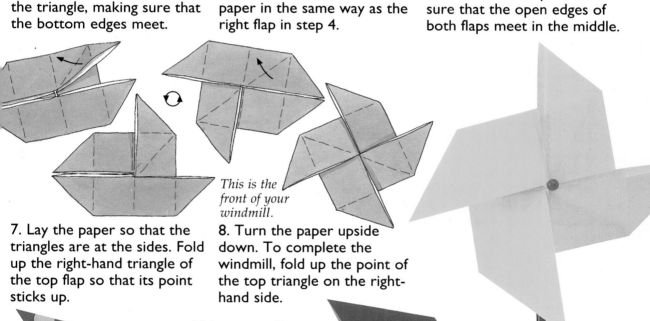

This is the front of your windmill.

7. Lay the paper so that the triangles are at the sides. Fold up the right-hand triangle of the top flap so that its point sticks up.

8. Turn the paper upside down. To complete the windmill, fold up the point of the top triangle on the right-hand side.

Make sure you blow at the open edges of the triangles.

To attach a windmill to a stick, see the opposite page.

You could paint the stick.

17

Beads

Origami beads are made up of two halves which are joined together. They can be made in lots of different sizes. **You will need**: two square pieces of paper, both the same size. The finished bead will be the same length as one side of the square. You could start with two pieces of paper, 10 x 10cm (4 x 4in). The finished bead will be 10cm (4in) long.

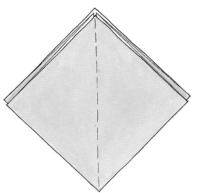

1. To make a half bead, first make a preliminary base, as shown on page 32, from one square of paper.

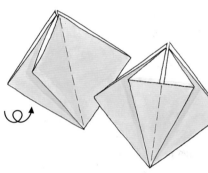

2. With the open ends of the paper at the top, lift the top flap on the left so that it sticks up in the air.

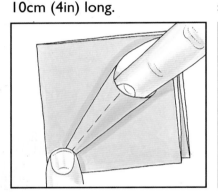

3. Now put your finger or a pencil inside the flap you just lifted to open it out. Remove your finger or the pencil.

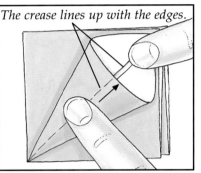

The crease lines up with the edges.

4. Now press down at the bottom of the flap and smooth carefully up, as shown in the picture above.

5. Turn the paper over and repeat steps 2-4 on the other side. Both sides of the paper now look the same.

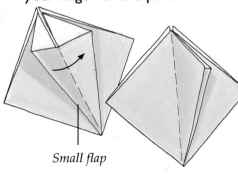

Small flap

6. Now fold the small flap on the left onto the one on the right. Make sure that the edges meet.

Large flap

7. Lift the large flap on the left, as in step 2, and repeat steps 3 and 4 very neatly to squash it flat.

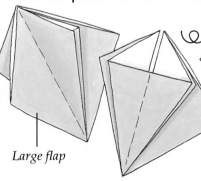

8. Turn the paper over and repeat steps 6 and 7 on the other side. Fan out all the flaps of the half bead evenly.

A chain of beads

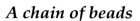

1. Cut a thin piece of wire, such as florists' wire, longer than each bead. The wire acts as a needle. Make a loop at one end.

2. Thread a long piece of thread through the loop and tie a big knot near the end. Thread a small plastic bead onto the thread.

3. With scissors, snip off the ends of each origami bead to make small holes to thread through.

4. Thread your beads together and tie on a plastic bead after the last one.

Pull the needle through very gently.

For necklaces and bracelets, leave some extra thread at both ends of a chain.

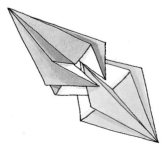

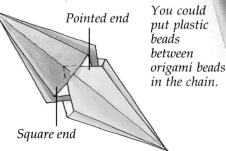

Pointed end

Square end

9. Make another half bead. When you have finished, fit the open ends of each half together roughly.

10. Now slot the pointed ends of each half into the square ends of the other. Fix one in at a time.

You could put plastic beads between origami beads in the chain.

Chains of shiny beads could be used to decorate your origami Christmas tree (pages 28-29).

Star box

These boxes can be used to store things or you could put presents in them for your family and friends. Try using double-sided paper, or glue two pieces of paper together. **You will need**: a square piece of paper. You could start with a piece 30 x 30cm (12 x 12in).

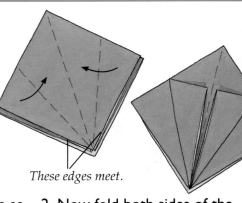

These edges meet.

1. Make a preliminary base as shown on page 32. When you have finished, turn it so that the open ends are facing you.

2. Now fold both sides of the top layer in so that they meet in the middle, as shown in the picture above.

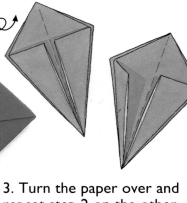

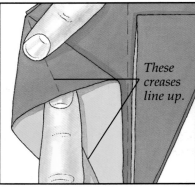

These creases line up.

3. Turn the paper over and repeat step 2 on the other side. Now unfold the left flap so that it sticks up in the air.

4. Open out the flap, by putting your finger inside. Squash the flap flat, starting from the top.

You could fill a box with party treats or pot pourri.

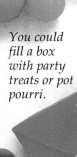

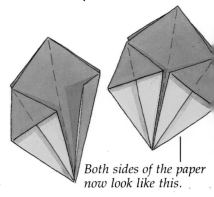

Both sides of the paper now look like this.

5. Lift the flap on the right and repeat step 4. Turn the paper over, open both flaps again, and squash them flat.

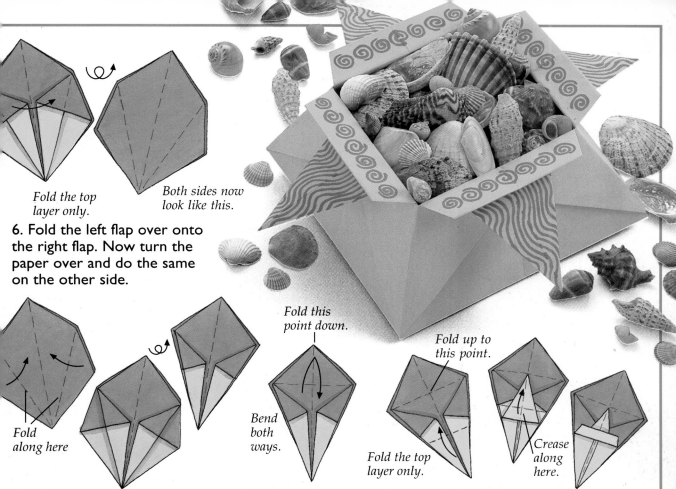

Fold the top layer only.

Both sides now look like this.

6. Fold the left flap over onto the right flap. Now turn the paper over and do the same on the other side.

Fold this point down.

Fold up to this point.

Fold along here

Bend both ways.

Fold the top layer only.

Crease along here.

7. Fold in the top layer, at both sides, along the diagonal creases. Turn the paper over and repeat on the other side.

8. Fold down the top of the paper and crease and unfold it. Fold it back the other way along the crease and unfold.

9. Fold the bottom flap up to the point shown above. Fold up the edge you have just creased as far as it will go.

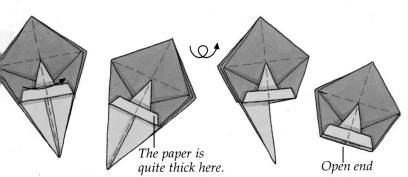

The paper is quite thick here.

Open end

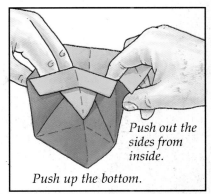

Push out the sides from inside.

Push up the bottom.

10. Now fold the left flap over onto the right, and repeat step 9 with the bottom flap.

11. Now turn the paper over and repeat steps 9 and 10. Make sure that all the bottom edges meet.

12. Hold the open end of the paper as shown. Pull the sides apart so that it looks like the finished boxes in the pictures.

21

Bombs away

When you fill this origami water bomb with water and throw it, it will explode and soak whatever target it hits. Make sure you use it outdoors as it's very messy.
You will need: a square piece of paper 21 x 21cm (8 x 8in) makes a bomb about 6cm (2½in) high. Gift wrap works very well.

You can only throw each water bomb once.

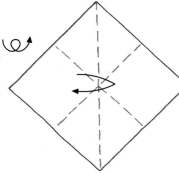

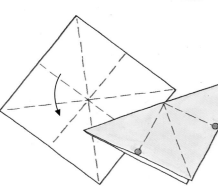

1. With the paper right side up, make two creases by folding opposite sides together and unfolding them.

2. Turn the paper over and place it so that one corner is facing you. Fold it in half from side to side and unfold.

3. Fold in half from top to bottom. Hold the paper in both hands at the spots marked in the picture above.

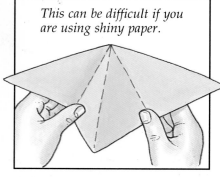

This can be difficult if you are using shiny paper.

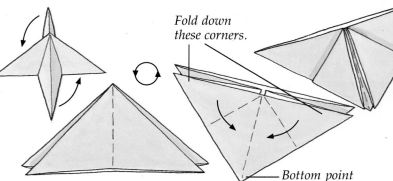

Fold down these corners.

Bottom point

4. Push the paper in so that your fingers meet in the middle. There are now four triangles sticking out.

5. Now fold the triangle in front to the right, and the triangle at the back to the left. Press the paper flat.

6. Place the paper with the long edge at the top. Fold the top corners of the top layer down to the bottom point.

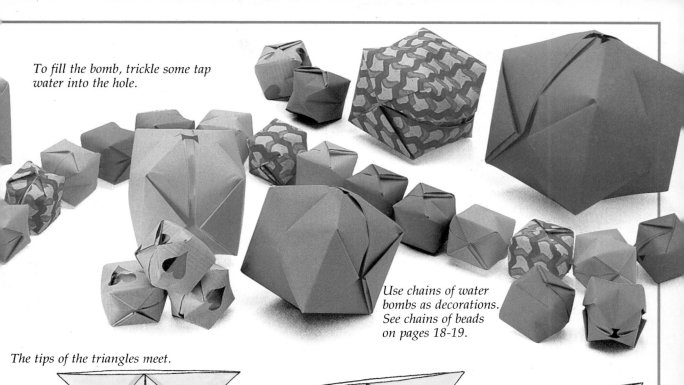

To fill the bomb, trickle some tap water into the hole.

Use chains of water bombs as decorations. See chains of beads on pages 18-19.

The tips of the triangles meet.

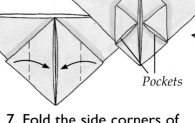

Pockets

7. Fold the side corners of the triangles made in step 6 into the middle. This makes little pockets shown above.

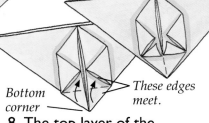

Bottom corner — These edges meet.

8. The top layer of the bottom corner has two points. Fold these points up along the dotted lines shown.

9. Fold the triangles shaded red above along their diagonal sides, up over the triangles with the pockets. Unfold.

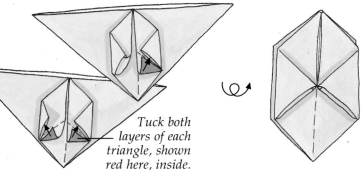

Tuck both layers of each triangle, shown red here, inside.

10. Lift the side triangles with the pockets. Open out the pockets a little. Tuck the triangles below them inside.

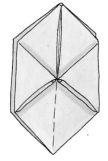

11. Now turn the paper over and repeat steps 6-10 very neatly. The paper now looks the same on both sides.

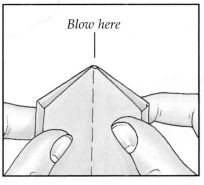

Blow here

12. Pull the two halves of the paper apart. Blow into the hole at the top to puff up the paper into a box shape.

23

Lily

These lilies can only be made from a square piece of paper, but you can make them in different sizes. The first time you make one, use the measurements given below, as the square of paper is fairly large and easier to fold than a smaller one.
You will need: a square piece of paper 24 x 24cm (10 x 10in); a pencil.

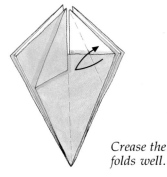

Crease the folds well.

1. Follow steps 1-8 of the bead on pages 18 and 19, but do not fan out the flaps. Lay the folded paper flat with the open ends at the top.

2. Fold the top layer of paper as shown in the picture above, so that the top sides meet in the middle. Now unfold them again.

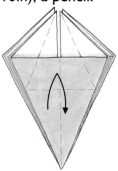

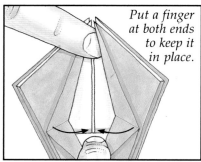

Put a finger at both ends to keep it in place.

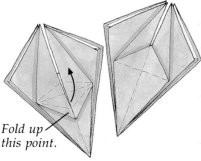

Fold up this point.

3. Now fold the bottom point up to the top point. Crease the fold well, as you are folding several layers of paper. Then unfold it again.

4. Put your fingers as shown and pull the top flap down so that the sides come inward, folding along the creases made in steps 2 and 3.

5. Make sure that the edges meet in the middle. Squash the paper flat. Fold the point shown above up toward the top of the paper and crease.

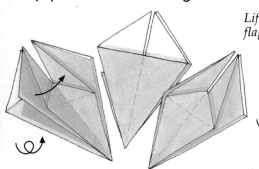

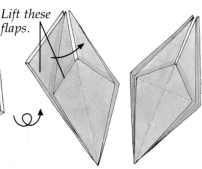

Lift these flaps.

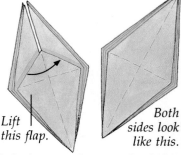

Lift this flap.

Both sides look like this.

6. Turn the paper over and repeat steps 2-4 on this side. Fold the top two flaps on the left over to the right and repeat steps 2-4 again.

7. Now turn the paper over, lift the top two flaps on the left over to the right, and repeat steps 2-4 very neatly on this side.

8. Lift the top flap on the left over onto the right. Turn the paper over and do the same on this side. The paper now looks the same on both sides.

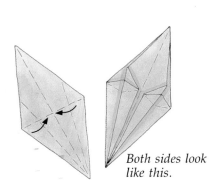

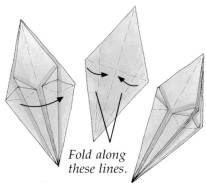

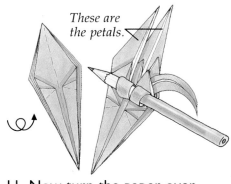

Both sides look like this.

Fold along these lines.

These are the petals.

9. Fold the bottom sides of the top flap into the middle. Turn the paper over and repeat this on the other side of the paper.

10. Fold the top two flaps on the left over to the right. Now fold the bottom sides of the top flap into the middle, along the diagonal lines.

11. Now turn the paper over and repeat step 10. Fan out all the flaps evenly, and curl the petals by rolling each one around a pencil from the top.

You can make a lily from very thin paper but fold it very gently.

For a stem, push the end of the lily into a fat straw that bends near the top.

Make several lilies and stand them in a vase.

Flapping bird

This flapping bird will flap its wings when you hold it at the base of the neck and pull its tail very gently. You could make chains of birds like the ones in the pictures on the opposite page.
You will need: a square piece of paper, 15 x 15cm (6 x 6in).

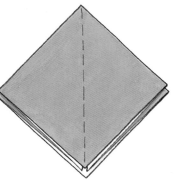

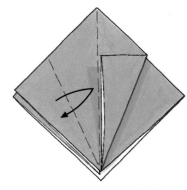

1. Make a preliminary base as shown on page 32. When you have finished, turn it so that the open ends are facing you.

2. Fold the sides of the top layer in to the middle so that the edges meet. Now unfold them again.

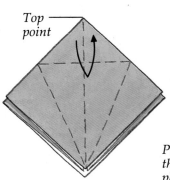

Top point

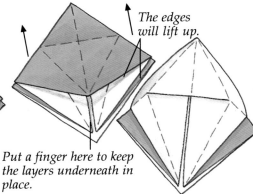

The edges will lift up.

Put a finger here to keep the layers underneath in place.

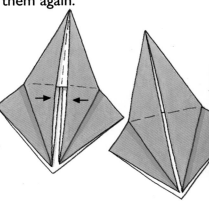

3. Fold the top point down and crease where the paper meets the top of the two diagonal creases. Unfold.

4. Lift the bottom corner of the top layer of paper over the top point, bending along the crease made in step 3.

5. Now fold the sides into the middle, along the creases made in step 2, creasing from the bottom.

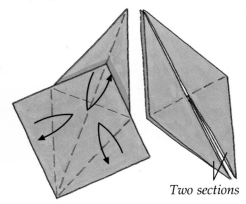

Two sections

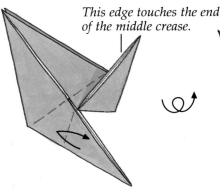

This edge touches the end of the middle crease.

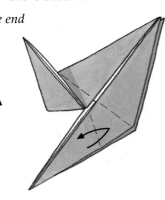

6. Turn the paper over and repeat steps 2-5 on this side. The bottom half of the paper has two sections.

7. Fold the bottom points up so that they stick out at an angle. Crease the folds well and then unfold them.

8. Turn the paper over and repeat step 7. Fold along the creases made on the other side of the paper.

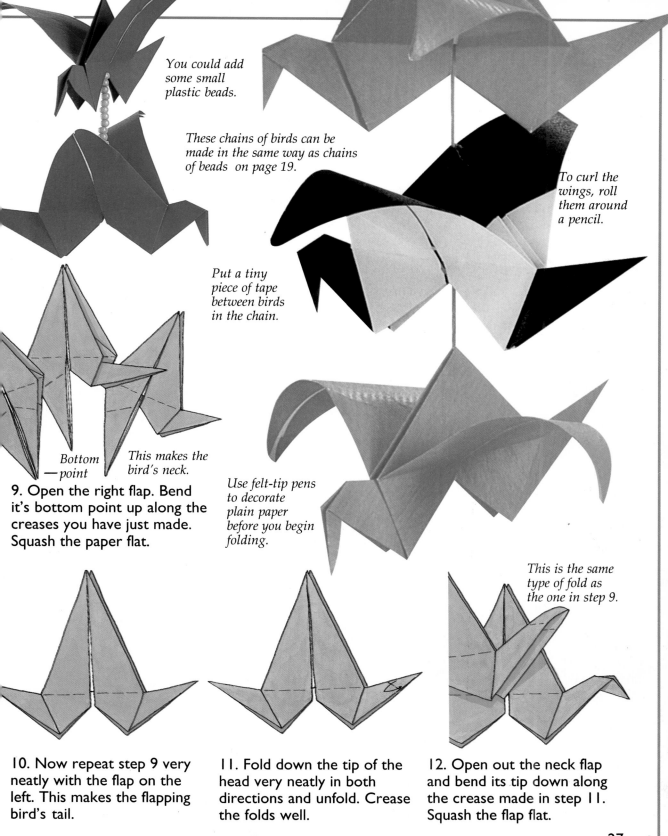

You could add some small plastic beads.

These chains of birds can be made in the same way as chains of beads on page 19.

To curl the wings, roll them around a pencil.

Put a tiny piece of tape between birds in the chain.

Bottom
— point

This makes the bird's neck.

9. Open the right flap. Bend it's bottom point up along the creases you have just made. Squash the paper flat.

Use felt-tip pens to decorate plain paper before you begin folding.

This is the same type of fold as the one in step 9.

10. Now repeat step 9 very neatly with the flap on the left. This makes the flapping bird's tail.

11. Fold down the tip of the head very neatly in both directions and unfold. Crease the folds well.

12. Open out the neck flap and bend its tip down along the crease made in step 11. Squash the flap flat.

Christmas tree

This tree has four sections. For each section, fold the paper into a preliminary base (page 32) before continuing with the steps below. Start with the open ends of each base facing you. **You will need**: four pieces of paper cut to these sizes:
1. 65 x 65cm (26 x 26in)
2. 50 x 50cm (20 x 20in)
3. 35 x 35cm (14 x 14in)
4. 20 x 20cm (8 x 8in)

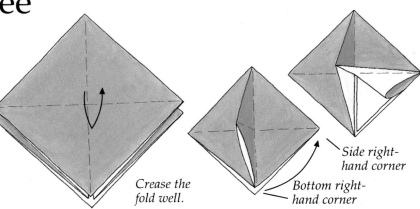

Crease the fold well.

Side right-hand corner

Bottom right-hand corner

1. Fold the preliminary base in half from top to bottom and unfold it again. Turn the paper over and repeat this.

2. Lift the left flap. Bring the bottom right-hand corner of this flap up to meet the side right-hand corner.

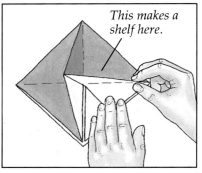

This makes a shelf here.

3. Hold all the corners on the right together very firmly and flatten the small triangular flap below the shelf.

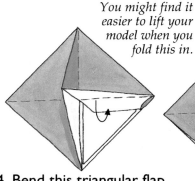

You might find it easier to lift your model when you fold this in.

4. Bend this triangular flap back under itself, so that it tucks in between the layers of paper above it.

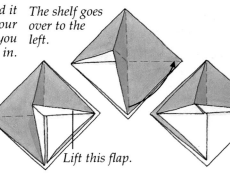

The shelf goes over to the left.

Lift this flap.

5. Lift the right flap over to the left and bring its bottom corner up to meet the right corner. Repeat steps 3 and 4.

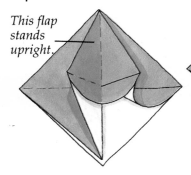

This flap stands upright.

6. Lay the paper so that the back of it is flat and lift the left flap. The shelves on the right are slightly squashed.

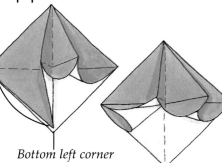

Bottom left corner

7. Bring the bottom left corner of the standing-up flap up to meet the side left-hand corner of the paper.

This is the top of the section.

8. Flatten the triangular flap as before, and tuck it into the layers above it. The paper now has three shelves.

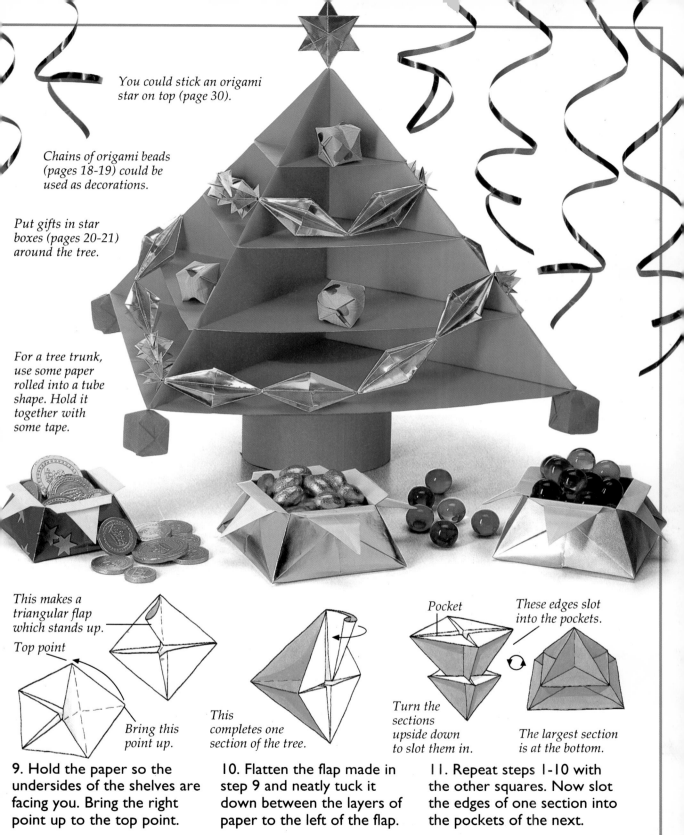

You could stick an origami star on top (page 30).

Chains of origami beads (pages 18-19) could be used as decorations.

Put gifts in star boxes (pages 20-21) around the tree.

For a tree trunk, use some paper rolled into a tube shape. Hold it together with some tape.

This makes a triangular flap which stands up.

Top point

Bring this point up.

This completes one section of the tree.

Turn the sections upside down to slot them in.

Pocket

These edges slot into the pockets.

The largest section is at the bottom.

9. Hold the paper so the undersides of the shelves are facing you. Bring the right point up to the top point.

10. Flatten the flap made in step 9 and neatly tuck it down between the layers of paper to the left of the flap.

11. Repeat steps 1-10 with the other squares. Now slot the edges of one section into the pockets of the next.

29

Star

You will need: a square piece of paper 15 x 15cm (6 x 6in).

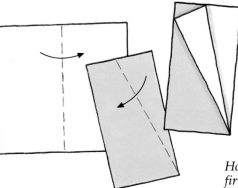

You will not need this piece.

Cut along here.

Hold the paper together firmly while cutting.

1. Fold the paper in half from left to right. Fold the top layer of the top right corner over to the left of the paper, and crease as shown.

2. Cut through both layers of paper along the left edge of the flap made in step 1. Continue with the bottom triangle only. Open it out.

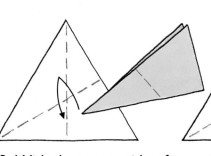

The middle point is where the creases mee[t]

3. With the wrong side of the paper facing up, fold the bottom right corner to the top, crease the fold well and unfold it again.

4. Fold the bottom left corner to the top. Unfold. Turn the paper over. Fold the three corners into the middle point shown above. Unfold.

Now fold and unfold the other corners.

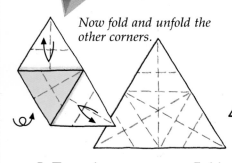

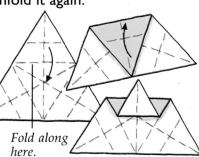

Fold along here.

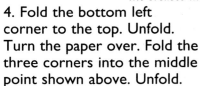

Left flap   Top flap

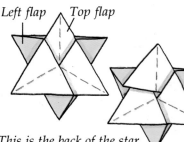

This is the back of the star.

5. Turn the paper over. Fold and unfold each tip across to the opposite side. Each tip touches the crease halfway along the opposite edge.

6. Fold one corner down along a crease made in step 5. Fold the point of this flap up along the crease almost halfway down the flap.

7. Repeat step 6 with the right and then the left corners of the paper. Tuck the top of the left flap under the flap at the top.

Other ideas

On this page you will find ideas for using some of the origami models that you have made in this book.

Greeting cards

You could make greeting cards from the flapping bird on pages 26-27 and the star on page 30. Use a rectangle of thin cardboard. Fold the rectangle in half with the short edges together.

Pencil tops

You could make these pencil tops from the water bombs on pages 22-23. Use a square piece of paper 9 x 9cm (4 x 4in). Poke a pencil up through the hole in the water bomb and decorate it using the ideas shown below. To attach the water bomb firmly, you could put some glue on the end of the pencil.

Glue a picture on the front to make a television. Add a piece of florists' wire on top.

·Make a cat by pulling out the top triangles from their pockets at the sides of a water bomb.

Glue the flapping bird or star to the front of the card.

Secret star card

You could write messages inside a star that stay hidden until the star is opened. Follow steps 1-5 of the star on page 30. Write a message between the red creases below, and then continue with the remaining steps. Glue the back of the star to a card.

Pull out each flap to reveal a message.

Use felt-tip pens and shiny paper if you want to make a strawberry, a robot or a funny face.

31

Preliminary base

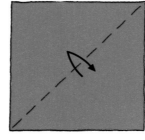

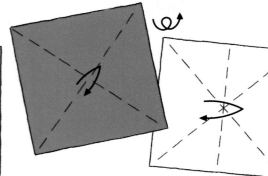

Lots of origami models begin by folding paper in the same way. This preliminary base is used as a starting point for the beads (pages 18-19), the star box (pages 20-21), the lily (pages 24-25), the flapping bird (pages 26-27) and the Christmas tree (pages 28-29). It can only be made from a square piece of paper.

1. Place the paper right-side up. Fold the bottom right corner up to the top left corner, crease and unfold.

2. Fold and unfold the bottom left corner to the top right corner. Turn it over. Fold the side edges together. Unfold.

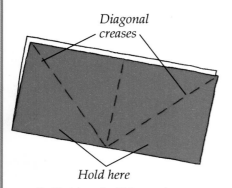

Diagonal creases

Hold here

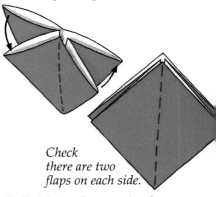

Check there are two flaps on each side.

3. Fold in half from bottom to top. Hold the bottom edge at both sides just below the diagonal creases.

4. Bring your fingers together so that the diagonal creases meet in the middle. Four triangles stick out, as shown.

5. Fold the flap at the front to the right, and the flap at the back to the left. Press the paper flat.

With thanks

Most of the projects in this book are traditional. The ones that are not have been designed by Sarah Goodall (Snake fangs), Nick Robinson (Crown), Makoto Yamaguchi (Christmas tree), Mitsuo Okuda (Fox family), George Jarschauer (Glider) and Lewis Simon (Star).
The instructions for the glider (pages 6-7) and the star (page 30) have been provided by Rick Beech.

Most of the origami models in the photographs in this book were made by Paul Jackson.
With thanks to Nadia Allman, Red and Kattja Madrell, Lewis Dasso and Jessica Roberts.